Ultimate Dead Baby Joke Book

The Ultimate Dead Baby Joke Book

From

Unearthed Books

ISBN-10:1461150914
ISBN-13: 9781461150916

Printed in the United States

CONTENTS

PREFACE

If you're reading this, means you have a twisted sense of humor. I can understand it because I wrote it.

I want you to laugh and be at ease. Sometimes we need to laugh at the most horrendous things we know of, otherwise, we would be hiding under our bed for all of eternity afraid to laugh at what scares us the most.

This book will be burnt up into nothing. It has no redeeming value or anything wise to say. The only thing it has is a gumption for those who need to laugh at death and the subversive.

We're not perfect. We are far from it but for us to laugh, at the most horrendous of horrors can help us to understand we are human. That laughter can sometimes destroy us and save us at the same time.

So lets have a laugh at the absurd and totally wrong. The rich and the famous and especially the nameless corporations that shove themselves down our throats every day.

Enjoy reading the jokes.

UNEARTHED BOOKS

The Ultimate Dead Baby Joke Book

1 - DEAD BABY JOKES

What do you call a dead baby put into an oven and cooked at 350 degrees, basted and stuffed?

Thanksgiving.

How many dead babies do you have to throw at a bear so it won't attack you.

Three.

How many dead babies does it take to float a crab trap?

One, unless it's skinny, then you have to use two.

What does a dead baby boy and a dead baby girl taste like?

The dead baby boy tastes like hickory and the dead baby girl tastes like vomit.

How many dead babies does it take to stop a shark attack?

Six, their hungrier then bears.

How many dead babies does it take to change a lightbulb?

Only one. A live baby has to hold the dead baby to unscrew the bulb, there by electrocuting itself to become a dead baby. Good thing is, we have two dead babies for one bulb.

What do you do if the cops show up at your house and find fifty three dead babies on your bed?

Run!

What is the best way to eat a dead baby?

Blanched and then fried. Meat is always so much more tender.

When trying to pick up a dead baby in the alleyway, what is the 1st thing you say?

"What's a sexy dead baby like you doing in a place like this."

If a freshly dead baby weighs seven pounds and an emaciated dead baby weighs three pounds. Why is there a difference?

Because you ate a couple of pounds when it was fresh.

Dead babies are like the stars in the sky.

Even if you can't see them all, you know they are more then you can count.

How many dead babies can you give to your lover on Valentines day?

Ones enough.

What do you get when you kill three babies and hang them over your fireplace.

A hard-on.

When juggling three dead babies, what is the rule?

Left to right… left to right.

What is the rule when you leave Santa Clause, cookies, milk and a dead baby?

Always chocolate chip.

When cooking a dead baby for the family over the holidays, what are you supposed to do?

Bring out the fine China.

When using dead babies as currency. How many Vietnamese dead babies are equal to one dead American baby?

One and a half… the exchange rate is pretty high.

In China, how much is one dead baby equal to an American dead baby?

Five to one. They kill all of the girl babies so there's a massive surplus.

If a politician kicked a dead baby across the road, what party do they belong to?

Republican.

How many hippies does it take to kill a baby?

All of them. It takes forever to kill it with crappy food and pot smoke.

How many dead babies does it take to make a raft to float from Cuba to the US?

Twenty Three. Their stomachs bulge from gasses given off while they decompose for better bouncy after twelve hours.

What do you do when you're in a restaurant and order the dead baby under glass?

Always order a side of Au jus. It always tends to be dry under glass.

How long do you marinate a ten-pound dead baby for a party of four?

Gordon Ramsey said three and a half hours, maximum. Any more would be fucking overkill.

How many dead babies can Regis Philbin eat?

Two and a half and they were very big babies.

If George Lucas made Star Wars with dead babies, what would it have been called?

Dead Babies.

If you think about dead babies all of the time. What do they call you?

In love.

When using a dead baby as a floaty in the pool. What should you always do?

The backstroke.

When poking a dead baby with stick, what should you always do?

Poke it gently.

If you had a hundred dead babies in a room with typewriters; how long would it take them to type out Shakespeare's Hamlet?

Forever. They're all dead.

Dead babies don't want a divorce.

They just want to be eaten.

If you cooked a dead baby in the oven, what is the most likely thing you will forget?

Cranberry sauce.

If Jerry had one dead baby and Jacob was about to steal two dead babies. What does that mean?

One in the hand is worth two in the cemetery plot.

If a dead baby is crunchy and stale, what did you probably do?

Left it out too long and overcooked it.

How do you cook a dead baby?

Butter… lots of butter with a hint of saffron and marmalade.

If Danny Bonuduce found a dead baby in an alleyway, what would he say?

"What's a sexy dead baby like you doing in a place like this?"

If the Fonz jumped a dead baby instead of a shark, what would it have been called?

AWESOME!

Dead baby eating is a contest in Tijuana Mexico.

I have a corporate box in the stadium with an open bar. Can you say priceless!

My dog got into my dead baby stash.

I had to wait twelve hours for my dog to give it back.

What's better? A dead baby in plastic wrap or a dead baby in a bag?

Plastic wrap… it always keeps it fresher.

2 - MORE DEAD BABIES

If a monkey was to kidnap a baby and kill it, what do you do?

Videotape it and stick it on Youtube so the rest of us can enjoy it.

If an incestuous serial killer has sex with a dead baby, what does he call him?

A brother from another mother.

How many maggots does it take to consume five whole babies?

I don't know. The maggots keep turning into flies and lay more eggs on the dead babies before I can finish counting them all.

If you're going to make slippers out of dead babies, what do you always have to remember?

Always cut off the head. Your big toe isn't that big.

When seasoning a two month old dead baby. What should you always remember?

1/4th Kosher Salt, ¼ th pepper and ½ Oregeno.

When eating the flesh of a dead baby in a high-class restaurant. What should you always remember?

The salad fork is always on the left. Never on the right.

What country has the lowest crime rate for dead babies?

Sweden… so don't go there.

In a Wall Street Journal poll: What is the leading name for dead babies?

Delicious.

If you made a roof for your house with dead babies, how many repairs would you need in three months?

Too many, babies rot all the time.

If you used a dead baby as bait on your next fishing trip. How many fish would you catch?

A shitload!

If Steven Speilberg made ET The Extra Terrestrial but with a dead baby. What would it have been called?

DB The Dead Baby.

How many dead babies can Brad Pitt eat?

Only one dead African baby. He's a picky eater.

If Apple sold dead babies via I-Tunes what would it be called?

I-Deadbaby.

If Willy Wonka can eat dead umpa lompa babies, how many can Oprah eat?

None, she doesn't own any dead umpa lumpa babies.

If Oprah gave out two hundred and fifty dead babies during one of her Oprah's Favorite Things Episode, what would happen?

You would still have to pay tax on it.

If Kate Gosselin's show was Kate plus eight dead babies. What would happen?

You would watch it more.

Obama vetoed a bill that gave us the right to eat dead babies.

I think we should repeal that one.

Bill Clinton not only had sex with Monica Lewinski but with a dead baby at the same time.

The reason you don't know about it is because the dead baby wasn't wearing a dress.

How does Rush Limbaugh eat dead babies?

Covered in maple syrup, cool whip and chocolate sprinkles.

Sears now includes dead baby transport with every crib.

Sears is always looking towards the future.

Rosie O Donnel admitted to eating a dead baby once.

It's okay, she was high at the time and in college.

Having sex with a dead baby is almost fruitless.

Unless you're bouncing it around, making its arms flail everywhere.

Having sex with a dead baby is wrong.

Unless it's on Monday Tuesday, Wednesday, Friday or Saturday. I didn't pick the days, they were just told to me.

Making underwear out of dead baby flesh is wrong!

Unless you use a Sears 431 cross-stitching sewing machine. Then it's all right.

Sometimes I wonder how I've gotten so many dead babies in my spare room.

Then I realize we all have to have hobbies.

If you take a dead baby and throw it against the wall, really hard.

You get the same splatter as the same fifty-three babies before it.

How many dead babies do you have to eat to cure cancer?

I don't know but we should ask Michael Douglas.

When John Wayne was having sex with a couple of dead babies. What happened?

I don't know. The Duke always made us look away.

Nailing three dead babies to my wall.

I realized I have a great fucking hobby.

Dead babies are like potato chips.

Once you had sex with one. You have to have sex with them all.

If a dead baby can talk while you're having sex with it. What would it say?

Owww, I'm not supposed to bend that way.

How many dead babies would it take to raise Shamu to the top of his aquarium?

Too many. I couldn't steal that many to find out before the guards came.

What's the difference between two dead porpoises and five dead babies?

Not much. They all feel the same.

How many ounces of dead baby guts does it take to make a decent pot of chili?

Thirty seven ounces. You always need more dead baby then beans.

Always tell your waiter to thank the cook when he brings you out dead baby bolognese.

It's a lot harder to cook then you think.

Always use a condom when having sex with a dead baby.

You don't know where it's been and you just know, it's a total slut.

Killing your first baby is like loosing your virginity.

It's totally awkward at first but you know you want to do it again and again and again…

Having sex with a dead baby in front of thirty people...

Can cost you a lot of money.

A dead babies skin is more luxurious then a seal's pelt.

That's more of a statement then a joke.

How many dead babies can a male lion eat?

Eight! They can eat more then a shark because they throw it back up for their cubs but they only throw up two babies because their still hungry. So actually, six, same as the shark.

3 - MANY MORE DEAD BABY JOKES

How many dead babies can I eat?

As many as I want. I use Dexatrim!

When using a turkey fat fryer to cook dead babies. How long does it take?

An hour and a half if you don't keep the giblets in it.

I trained a couple of dead babies to do tricks.

Sit, play dead and hold your breath. That's all I can do without forcing it to play anal rape.

Surprisingly, the Catholic Church refuses to molest dead babies.

It's missing out on a real good thing.

If you have ten baby legs and eight buns for hotdogs; what do you do with the extra two baby legs?

Give them to Jose. It's always fun to watch him eat off the bone.

If a cop finds you having sex with a dead baby corpse.

Maybe you shouldn't do it outdoors!

Dead babies are like macaroni and cheese.

Once you take a bite, you love it.

Killing a baby is not the end of the world.

It's the start of a nutritious breakfast.

A dead baby farm is something that should be appreciated.

At least that's what the farmer told me.

Bloated rotten corpses under 6 months of age are considered legal in California.

I think we should move there!

I can no longer take dead babies out for trick or treating.

Their heads only hold six ounces of treats and I can only carry three at a time.

I can't find dead babies at Wal-mart.

I guess I got to go to Publix from now on.

The Situation has never had sex with a dead baby.

I'd hate to see his contract!

MTV wanted a show with a lot of dead babies.

I contacted them and they didn't want that many dead babies. I guess reality shows are not really reality. But I got a call from Snooki afterwards.

Robert De Niro thought about having sex with a dead baby but decided against it.

Good thing... more for us.

A dead baby is like a lilac in the spring.

They're all over the place.

Finding Dead Baby formula in the store is like finding a five pound package of bacon.

Awesome and totally needed!

Don't use crab and shrimp boil to cook your dead babies with.

It shrinks them and makes them taste like seafood. No one wants a dead baby to taste like that.

How do you make love to a decomposed baby.

Very carefully and I do mean... very carefully.

When dressing a dead baby for your high school reunion. Always go with grey.

Always.

If a baby is choking to death on a toy. What should you do?

Thank Toys R Us!

Denny's has a new breakfast called the toddler express. I am still waiting on my grilled dead baby but these cheese hashbrowns are to die for.

Sort of like the baby I'm waiting on.

David Schwimmer always needed one dead baby to fuck so he could prepare for his roll of Ross on friends.

David Schwimmer is an actor of the highest caliber.

How do you French kiss a dead baby?

Very, very slowly.

Carrot Top has a Vegas show where he juggles dead babies. He drops them a lot.

He needs to stay off the steroids.

If you play tug of war with a decomposed baby. What happens?

Usually a mess.

How many dead babies does it take to fill your pants.

I don't know, I only have seven dead babies on me so lets see if they will fit.

Julia Childs once wrote a cookbook for cooking dead babies.

It's the best book on the planet.

Marlon Brando once worked with a dead baby.

I know, I envy him too.

What's the biggest problem of trying to eat a dead baby when you're a teenager?

It keeps getting stuck in your braces.

What do you call it when the cops find a dead baby and send it to the morgue?

A waste.

Marco Polo found a dead baby once.

He had to travel half way around the world to find it. That's dedication.

They found over a thousand dead babies in a Buddhist temple.

No wonder Buddhists are so peaceful.

What do you call a dead baby in your attic?

A keepsake.

How many dead babies does it take to feed a football team.

Fifty two; because the damn water boy ain't getting any.

What's the best thing about a Siamese dead baby?

Double blowjobs.

How much broken glass can you stuff into a dead baby.

I'll be right back and let you know.

If a lion and a tiger are both eating dead babies. Which on will finish 1st?

I don't know but it would be awesome to watch.

Remember to always remove the net on a hoop when you're playing basketball with a dead baby.

Their arms and legs get stuck in the net too much and who wants to stop the game to pull out the ladder every couple of minutes.

When the game of football was 1st introduced, they used dead babies instead of footballs.

It didn't last long because someone would always eat it within the 1st five minutes.

Never stick a dead baby in a microwave.

It always comes out too rubbery.

How much flavor does a barbecued baby have?

Just enough to want seconds.

If Justin Timberlake ate a rotten dead baby on the way to the airport; how many vomit bags would he need for the flight?

Just one and he would call it a doggie bag.

I have never seen Andrew Zimmerman eat a dead baby on his TV show.

I guess he doesn't want to show you he keeps the good stuff at home.

Snoop Doggy Dog tried to smoke a dead baby once.

Just once and he's still high.

In Texas the 1st International Baby Cook Off begins next summer.

It's going to be so confusing because no one is going to know whether or not to eat em or fuck em or fuck em then eat em. Either way I already bought my tickets.

Beyonce bought a baby for Jay Z for his fortieth birthday. She killed it and then watched it rot for a month and then gave it to him.

Jay Z wasn't happy because he missed all the fun.

Abraham Lincoln was talking about dead babies during the Gettysburg Address.

People thought different so they freed the slaves.

What's funnier then a dead baby impaled on a pole.

Not much

4 - TOO MANY DEAD BABY JOKES

How many frozen dead babies can I stick in my freezer?

I'm up to fifty-two so far.

Try not to get your tongue stuck on a frozen dead baby.

It's embarrassing.

Always thaw out your dead frozen babies before you try to play with them.

Always.

How deep can you French kiss a dead baby.

I don't know, how long is your tongue?

How many tattoos can you tattoo on a dead rotten baby?

Not many. The skin keeps falling off.

How many babies can you stick in a blender?

I don't know. I prefer them whole.

Gomer Pyle of the United States Marine Corp had the most beautiful voice you have ever heard.

It was his diet of liquefied babies that made his voice sound Angelic to the ear.

Santa Clause does not like dead babies.

Every Christmas I leave him one and he only ever takes one bite.

The Easter Bunny loves dead babies.

Don't ask me how I know, I just know.

St Patrick's Day celebrates St. Patrick banishing all of the snakes out of Ireland.

It was because the damn snakes were eating everyone's dead babies and somebody had to do something.

If you were to stick a dead baby under your pillow; the Tooth Fairy would leave you a thousand dollars.

Dead babies are worth more then a thousand dollars so who would want to do that?

I've never seen a rotten dead baby at the flea market.

The collectors market on these things is insane.

I bought three dead babies off of eBay but instead, received three dead puppies in the mail.

I gave him the worst feedback ever.

Hardee's has a new rotten dead baby sandwich for the new kids meal.

The toy surprise is a rattle. They're very collectible.

Ronald McDonald has never had sex with a dead baby.

I don't know what he's waiting for.

Princess Leia gave birth to a still born and Luke Skywalker was very happy.

I mean really, who wants to have sex with a dead baby Ewok.

Travelocity should change their mascot from a garden gnome to a mutilated dead baby.

More people would go thru the TSA pat downs if they knew a dead mutilated baby was waiting for them in their hotel room.

Always wait to eat a cooked baby after you take it out of the oven.

You don't want to burn the roof of your mouth.

Marilyn Monroe tried to have sex with a dead baby boy.

It didn't work because its arms and legs were broken.

Why did Michael Moore eat five dead babies at one sitting?

He was mad at Rush Limbaugh.

Michael Moore tried to do a documentary on the dead baby market but couldn't get access?

No one wanted a liberal eating that many dead babies on film because all it would do is make them hungry.

Glenn Beck had sex with twenty two dead baby boys in one day.

It would have been twenty-three but he had to go to a tea party convention.

Glenn Beck loves dead baby boys.

You can always tell when he cries.

Glenn Beck tried to eat a dead baby girl once.

He couldn't finish it because he ate five dead baby boys an hour before.

What's the difference when Glenn Back eats a peach or a dead baby boy.

He doesn't cum on the peach before he eats it.

How many Republicans mutilate dead rotten babies for the fun of it?

All of them.

When using a dead baby as a pillow, how often are you supposed to wash it?

Never. Everyone knows you're not supposed to wash dead babies.

How many dead babies does it take fill my closet?

Sixty three. It's a small closet.

Have you ever played catch with a dead baby head?

No, here's the mitts, I'll get the ball.

Did you hear that Little Wayne tried to have sex with a dead baby but couldn't do it?

I knew he's all talk and no action.

The rapper Ludicris loves dead babies for breakfast, lunch and dinner.

He's a great artist.

Charlie Chaplain once made a movie about dead babies.

It's in the Smithsonian now.

Dead baby, dead babies, rotten dead babies and mutilated dead babies.

That's not a saying, it's my shopping list.

37

They tried to open up a brothel for dead babies in Las Vegas but it was denied.

I guess we can't call it sin city anymore.

Zales doesn't sell their golden encrusted ½ carat diamond dead baby heads for anniversaries anymore.

Don't shop at Zales.

On Black Friday, none of the stores ever have sales on dead babies.

They know people will pay for the good stuff.

How long can you bowl with a dead baby before it falls apart?

Two games.

Where do you drill the holes in your dead baby so you can bowl with it.

You don't, it already has three holes.

How many dead babies does Cher eat so she continues looking as good as she does.

Two a day.

When having a party and you're serving dead baby legs and arms as appetizers and cooking rotten dead baby as the entrée. What is the biggest complaint you get.

Where's the dead baby dessert?

When drinking dead baby blood that you siphoned out of five dead babies. What is the biggest complaint?

It always stains your teeth.

What kind of vitamins do you ingest when you eat a dead babies brain?

All of them.

The Surgeon General has sent out a press release that states, "Eating a dead baby is like a super meal that encompasses all four food groups."

That's sort of funny because we already knew that.

How many dead baby skeletons does it take to build a patio set?

Three hundred and twelve, maybe twelve more because I want to make a footstool.

How come you never see anyone use a dead baby as a flag?

They don't flap around enough for anyone's tastes.

How hard is it to blow up a dead baby like a balloon?

Really hard.

How many rotten, decomposing, dismembered babies can you fit into a tool shed?

I don't know. It's really hard to count them when they're all dismembered like this.

If you peel a dead babies skin off, how much sewing material do you get?

Not enough to make a pair of pants, I'll tell you that.

5 - FAMOUS DEAD BABY JOKES

How many dead baby farts, did Mario Lopez have to suck out off three dead babies assholes to get his job at Extra?

Twenty two, but he did three more to show them he would go the EXTRA mile.

How do you stop a dead baby from blowing up from internal gasses as the body rots?

Shishkabobs.

On Gilligan's Island, what episode did the Professor find Gilligan having sex with a dead baby?

All of them, all of the scenes ended up on the cutting room floor.

If Ginger and Mary Ann from Gilligan's Island had a threesome with a dead baby, what would it be called.

Totally awesome.

If you squish a dead baby with a car and run over it multiple times. What is it called?

A broken sex toy.

If Gene Simmons videotaped himself having sex with three rotten mutilated babies. What would you do?

You certainly wouldn't watch it. Who in the Hell wants to see Gene Simmons fuck?

Gene Simmons was supposed to eat a dead baby but he didn't.

He hired Eric Carr to do it.

Eric Carr was supposed to eat the same dead baby but he hired Vinny Vincent to do it.

Vinny Vincent was supposed to eat it but he hired Mark St John to do it.

Mark St. John was supposed to but he hired Bruce Kulick to do it.

Bruce Kulick refused because the dead baby was really rotten by the time he got to it.

They fired Bruce. Peter Criss and Ace Frehley enjoyed their dead baby, marinated in the blood of innocence over a candle lit dinner just to get back into the band that is called Kiss for a couple years. I guess crack is expensive.

Politically correct dead babies can't ever be a reality.

The Democrats want everyone to have access and the Republicans, want them for themselves. That's why I'm a Democrat.

Sometimes, a dead baby can lift your spirits.

It can't lift anything else because it's dead.

Dead babies are like the wind.

You can never see them all but sometimes, you can feel them on your face.

Wal-Mart had a sale on dead babies. It was huge and they didn't have enough to sell to everyone.

Abortion clinics always have a surplus. Their line is ten minutes. Even though Wal-Mart is cheaper, I'd rather go for speed then cheap.

Wal-mart uses cheap Chinese dead babies for their sales.

Always buy American!

Wal-mart began using cheap dead babies to feed America

Only buy free range dead babies over captivity dead babies. It just tastes better.

If you dress a dead baby in stocking and in lingerie. What would you call it?

Fucking hot!

If Latoya Jackson had sex with a rotten dead baby boy. What would you call it

Disgusting! No one wants to see a plastic surgery retard doing something beautiful.

How many dead babies did Mark McGwire squeeze into liquid to shoot up to become the Home Run World Record Holder?

As many as he could find.

Barry Bonds is known for shooting up steroids from mutilated dead babies.

It's why he's a great athlete!

Michael Vick tried to have dead baby fighting ring. It didn't work as well as the dogs. Why?

Everyone knows dead babies don't fight. They just lay there, wanting to get fucked.

Dead babies are like flowers blooming in the night.

You need to pick it before it closes its stamen,

Rotten dead babies are like standing in a line.

You hate the wait but it's totally worth it.

When you make a chorus line with a hundred dead babies. What do you get?

A musical that's actually worth the money.

When a hot dog stand sells dead baby legs.

The damn thing is always sold out by lunch.

If George Costanza ordered a dead baby for lunch.

You just know he's going to complain about it no matter how delicious it is.

Disney has a law, in their by-laws about fucking dead babies in their corporate charter.

Don't ever do it on Disney property.

Walt Disney didn't make Disney for fun or money.

He made it to fuck dead, mutilated babies.

Walt Disney used dead baby eyes for Bambi.

Inspiration comes from many different places.

Walt Disney made Dumbo as an inspiration for dead baby fucking.

It's all in black and white. Just read the credits.

Mickey Mouse has never had sex with a dead baby.

Minney Mouse is an over-bearing bitch!

Donold Duck tried to deep throat twenty dead babies, one after another.

No wonder his larynx was fucked up.

Goofy was so stupid, that he tried to eat a dead baby backwards.

Everyone knows you got to start at the head.

Papa John's uses dead babies on their pizza.

Just always ask for the baby meat lovers.

The Chinese Government has made it legal to eat girl babies.

I'm still not going there because baby girls taste like vomit.

If you were to make dead baby tacos for 4 people. How many dead babies would it take.

One, but everyone would still be hungry,

If you poured vodka into a baby like a watermelon. How much dead baby would you need to drink to get a buzz?

Not much, dead babies are filled with alcohol already.

Elvis Presley loved prescription drugs. He also loved dead babies.

You can tell by his song, "Love me tender."

Jim Morrison had a mystical experience with a dead baby once.

He wrote the Soft Parade the next day.

Led Zeppelin had the opportunity to fuck many rotten dead babies while they were together but they didn't.

They already sold their soul to the devil so they didn't have too.

Lars Ulrich fucked a dead baby in its ass.

It was a lot easier then suing Napster.

Glamour magazine is all about the baby fucking.

I never knew until I read the chapter on fucking dead baby boys.

Corporations are evil in our country. They tell us what we want but they never tell us what we need!

We really need dead baby sexy info. I never know what to do with my thumbs.

So last January, Glamour magazine finally told me what to do with my thumbs.

The dead baby I tried it on gave me a look, "Like, what the fuck?"

Time wrote a story on dead baby fucking. I was their lead story and told them everything. They twisted it like a normal story and suddenly I was rescuing babies.

A big media piece should get me more dead babies. Not more live ones!

We had to kill all of the babies we received from Time Magazine. It's not like we didn't enjoy it but I wasn't expecting this much work.

When cooking dead babies in a stew, never forget the mushrooms

Mushrooms always capture the taste of the stock,

When you break a dead infants jaw and realize you can have deep throat whenever you want. What do you do?

Call all of your friends so they can watch.

6 - SICKENING DEAD BABY JOKES

How much make up can you put on a dead baby.

All of it, their eyes don't water when you stuff your cock all the way down.

How many inches of cock can you stuff into a dead baby.

Six and a half. Anymore, you need to be fucking dead prostitutes.

If you have a dead prostitute and a dead baby on the same bed. What would you rather fuck?

The dead baby, dead prostitutes can't do kegals anymore.

How long do a couple of rotten dead babies have to wait to cross the street?

Forever, the crossing guards don't pay attention to them because they're dead.

How many High School Sports have dead babies in them?

Just track and field. It makes the javelin throw that much more exciting.

How much does it cost for Disneyland to have a gay mutilated baby parade?

Not much. Gays really don't want to see mutilated babies paraded around for their amusement.

If Amelia Arheart crossed the Atlantic to eat dead babies, what would have happened?

She would have made it.

Why did the Hindenburgh explode?

It only had one dead baby in it.

How many dead babies signed the Declaration of Independence?

Six, because no body really paid any attention.

If you take one dead baby and mutilate it and stuff it into a test tube, what would you call it besides delicious?

Filling!

If you take two dead babies and mix it with whip cream and stuff it into a pie. What would you call it.

The special of the day.

A dead baby in a jockstrap would be called?

A scene in Revenge of the Nerds that was cut.

If a dead baby told Vladimer Putin what to do. What would it be called?

Dmitry Medvedev.

If Henry Kissinger ate a dead baby with thyme and Rosemary with baked potatoes and asparagus, what would it be called?

Really good and I mean really good.

If John Travolta fucked and ate a dead baby today. What would it be called?

A waste, John Travolta doesn't need to eat dead babies anymore to further his career!

Miley Cyrus smoked a dead baby once to get high.

She didn't need too, everyone knows, you eat the dead baby for a thrill. You shoot up the dead baby to get high.

The Jonas Bros. tried to screw a dead baby but it didn't work.

Viagra boys… Viagra!

I tried to make a dead baby stew once but it didn't work out.

Where am I supposed to get eighteen dead baby kidneys for ½ a pound of potatoes? The ratio is beyond me!

I can only stuff two dead babies in my pants at one time.

Lets be thankful for stretchy pants!

If the fire department, comes to my house, because the house is on fire. What should I do?

Piss on all of the dead babies because I don't want to loose them all!

If I'm, pissing on all of the dead babies in my house, because the fire department is here to put out the fire. What should I do?

Try to kick them into a corner because they might not see them while I piss on them!

If I have 43 dead babies in my house and the house is on fire and I have over thirteen fireman trying to put it out but it's not going out. What should do?

Fucking run!

If a dead baby is served to us at Applebee's. What should you do.

Ask for more ranch because everyone knows the dead babies at Applebees are served dry.

If Matt Stone and Trey Parker didn't eat dead babies while fucking them in the mouth. What would happen?

South Park would be in re-runs!

How many dead babies did Matt Parker and Trey Stone have sex with to come up with South Park?

Only one and it was hilarious.

I tried to have sex with a dead baby and then tried to hook it up to raise up the flag pole because Sarah Palin is coming to town.

I guess you can call me patriotic.

How many tea party candidates are fucking dead babies?

None, because that's the Republican slogan.

How many lobbyists does it take to make a dead baby air tight?

Two and you don't see what the lobbyists do to get the job done.

How many good chef's use fennel when cooking a dead baby ?

To many, fennel doesn't really preserve the flavor!

Why doesn't Angelina Jolie like dead babies.

Because she can't adopt one.

How many dead babies does it take to fill a swimming pool.

A lot more then I can kill, I can tell you that.

If your wife ever finds you making love to a dead baby, what should you do?

Ask her to join you.

If you ever find a puppy playing with a dead baby, what should you do?

Hit it on the nose with a newspaper.

If you were to find your gardener having sex with your dead baby in the bushes, what should you do?

Get a new gardener.

If you ever overcook a dead baby, don't worry too much.

It still tastes delicious.

A super bowl party where they have dead baby BBQ is called?

A block party and a great place to be.

In Nebraska, they use dead babies to fertilize their corn crops.

No wonder the Jolly Green Giant is green.

How many dead babies does it take to feed a wedding of 120 people?

Fifteen fat ones or twenty two skinny ones.

How much stuffing can you stuff into an eight pound dead baby boy?

Four cupfuls.

7 - TRULY OFFENSIVE DEAD BABY JOKES

Mark Zuckerberg sent a friend request to a dead baby once.

It was never accepted because it was dead.

If you ever find a grizzly bear eating a dead baby, what should you do?

Walk the other way.

What would you do if you saw the same grizzly having sex with a dead baby?

Videotape it from a distance.

L. Ron Hubbard had sex with a dead baby once.

Scientology was written the next day.

If you had one hundred dead babies in your closet, what are you doing?

Saving for a rainy day.

How mushy does a dead baby get after you boil it?

Not too mushy that you can't eat it.

If Axl Rose had sex with a couple of dead babies?

Chinese Democracy would have been better.

What is the difference between a dead manatee's skin and a dead baby's skin?

One is silky smooth and the other is rough but oh so luxurious.

How many dead babies can a manatee eat?

None, everyone knows manatees are vegetarians.

If you stick a dead baby under your hat, what is it called?

High fashion.

If I left a dead baby in the trunk of your car, what would you do?

Probably nothing because you like the smell.

How many crazy straws can you stick into a fresh dead baby?

I don't know but I'm up to 47 so far.

If you were to find a dead baby wearing stockings and a garter belt in your hotel room, what would you do?

Quickly put out the Do Not Disturb sign.

Never use steam to wash your rotten dead babies with.

I think everyone can agree they look cuter with wrinkles.

How many dead babies can my wife eat?

None, she never wants to eat them with me!
Says, "It's a guy thing."

Ronald Reagen never ate a dead baby in his life.

Its because he had Nancy to eat.

How many trays of ice cubes can you make using
baby blood from one baby?

Never as many as I would like, I'll tell you that
much.

If the Fonze jumped dead babies instead of a
shark, how many do you think he could jump?

As many as you can line up in a row.

How many dead babies did it take to feed all of
those Chilean Miners that were stuck in a mine?

Way too many.

Japan has started to make dead baby robots last month.

Japan is always the leaders of industry.

Someone tried to make a dead baby sex toy once.

It never caught on because they could never get it to smell like the real thing.

Coca Cola once used dead baby blood for their original formula.

They had to chance it because they couldn't keep up with the orders.

If Cinemax started making erotic movies with dead babies, what would you do?

Order Cinemax as fast as you can and make sure you have enough lubrication for a week.

Discovery tried to show a dead baby pageant on TV but it didn't really work out.

Because none of the fathers of the dead babies wanted to leave the dressing room, you can imagine why.

Dead baby pageants can be grossly offensive.

Who wants to see them exploited by their mothers like that?

The only real complaint I have about a dead baby pageant is this…

Too much sparkly stuff and cowboy boots.

What do the judges give to the winner of a dead baby contest?

Ten minutes with an agent in a closet.

What do the judges give to the second runner up of a dead baby contest?

Twenty minutes with a agent in a closet. Runner ups always have to work harder then winners.

When you want to cook a dead baby, why should you always think of Burger King?

The whole, have it your way and flame broiled is always the way to go.

What's red, blue and pulsating?

My cock as I hold a dead baby.

Never use a dead baby to try to sharpen your ice skates with.

The skates never get sharp and it just mutilates your dead baby.

What's the difference between a fresh dead baby, a dead baby, a rotten dead baby, a mutilated dead baby, an emaciated dead baby and a skeletal dead baby?

Monday, Tuesday, Wednesday, Thursday, Friday and Saturday. Never on Sunday because Saturday is threesome night.

If it takes 10 pounds of pressure to pull your own ear off, how many pounds does it take to pull a dead baby's head off?

Way to little. Always remember to holds onto its shoulders when having sex with it.

Always remember to slowly rotate a dead baby on a shish kabob when cooking on a barbeque grill.

Nobody wants half burnt dead baby even though it still tastes amazing.

Always try to use low heat when making dead baby shish kabobs.

I know it's hard to do because who in the Hell wants to wait that long to eat.

Never eat your dead baby before Valentines Day. Always wait until after the holiday.

The sex is just that much more amazing on Valentines Day. Trust me.

Guess how many dead babies I can juggle after a couple of beers?

Surprisingly five! And usually I can only juggle three tennis balls but the floppy arms make it easier I guess.

I don't mean to brag when I say I have a membership to Columbia House; Dead Baby buy 3 for $1.00 deal.

You're right, I am bragging! I bought 3 for $1.00!

If Brent Bozell the Third, upright Conservative Republican commentator of the morality of the US ate 6 honeyglazed dead babies at one sitting, what would you call him?

A fucking pig!

How does Brent Bozell the Third keep his beard red?

It's red from the blood of dead babies and also a wonderful flavor savor.

How do you know Brent Bozell the Third eats dead babies?

Because he's a conservative republican.

Why does Brent Bozell the Third eat dead girl babies?

Because he loves the taste throw up.

If Brent Bozell, Glenn Beck and Rush Limbaugh ate a candlelit dinner of roasted dead baby but it was poisoned by the liberal media. What does that mean?

Well, it's a good start for one and the other, they knew it was coming from those damn liberals.

If our Government let us know they eat dead babies.

At least there would be some transparency in Government.

Toys R Us stopped selling clothes for dead babies.

Guess it's eBay for me.

Always try to find the dead baby diapers over normal baby diapers for your dead baby.

When they leak that much out of their assholes, you need a lot more absorbency.

How many more dead baby jokes can you read without praying to God to forgiveness?

None, you probably did as soon as you picked up this book.

How many dead baby jokes can come out of my mind?

About sixty more pages so lets pray for me, please.

If Jack Tripper from Three's Company had two dead babies instead of Chrissy and Janet what would have happened?

It would probably still be in production.

8 - DEAD BABIES IN POLITICS

If Seth McFarlane from Family Guy fame had an episode about dead babies and even had a musical number with Stewie and Brian and a dead baby, what would happen?

BEST EPISODE EVER! Guaranteed.

Why hasn't Seth McFarlane done a dead baby episode yet?

His finger isn't on the pulse anymore.

Quentin Tarintino has never made a movie about dead babies yet.

Give it time, nothing says action like a bunch of flailing dead baby arms and baby necrophilia.

I actually heard two dead baby jokes on the TV show Cougar Town... fucking... last week! Would you believe that?

Serendipity and finger on the pulse all at the same time.

I know the dead baby thing is getting bigger by the day you know. Everywhere I turn, dead baby this and dead baby that.

It's going to make collecting so much harder that I'm going to have to dip into my 401k.

Collecting dead babies is a different kind of hobby.

You can collect them, have sex with them, eat them and even make furniture out of them and even save your life by throwing them at predators. It's the best hobby EVER!

If this dead baby stem cell research thing really catches on, what are you going to do?

Suck a lot of dick to keep your fix going.

I tried to make a nursery mobile out of dead babies but it didn't really work.

It kept dripping on the baby.

Ronald Reagan ate a dead baby once even though he got to eat Nancy all the time. When he finally did, what happened?

The Berlin Wall came down.

When George Bush Sr. ate a dead baby at a highly established dinner in China with world leaders, what happened?

He puked all over himself. What did you really think that was, sushi?

Do you want to know why Keanu Reeves was that sad eating his sandwich?

It was the last of his dead baby brain pate and he knew Columbia House wouldn't deliver him any more for a month.

I just found out you can cook and shoot up dead baby eyeballs and get really high but not so high, your teeth are wriggling in your mouth.

It's not really a joke, just a future reference for you.

So I've been shooting dead baby eyeballs into my veins for about a month now.

The vein is a little red but I got to tell you. I think I found the perfect drug.

I think I made the discovery of a lifetime. You don't Jones for dead baby eyeballs because you can eat them after the eyeballs are gone.

I figure, the rest of the dead baby might be like methadone because you're still keeping it in your bloodstream.

So my friend's grandmother died recently and he said he found ten dried out dead fetuses in his Grandmother's attic.

It must be nice to find expensive antique heirlooms like that.

If you're stuck out at sea in a life raft and you only have two dead babies to feed five people, what do you do?

Eat the Mexicans first.

Steven Spielberg approached me the other day because he heard of my work on the dead baby joke book and asked to option it for a movie.

He gave me the pitch and talked about this sci-fi action adventure theme he had in mind. I looked at him and said... You're missing the point Stephen. It's a about a deep love and food, sort of like Eat, Pray, Love.

Jack Lalanne had a juicer for dead babies but it was specifically made to juice rotten dismembered babies.

It didn't sell well because once you start dismembering them, you can juice them yourself.

Rachel Ray's favorite meat is dead baby.

Succulent, easy to cook and it always looks great on her cooking show.

What's dead and small and spread all over your bed?

A dead baby, what did you think I was going to say. A dead squirrel?

How many dead babies does it take to change a tire?

I know; it's a silly question. Everyone knows dead babies can't change tires.

When George Washington was asked if he chopped down that cherry tree, what did he say?

I cannot tell a lie. I ran out of babies to dismember.

Thomas Jefferson loved to have sex with his slaves and dead babies.

He was better off with the dead babies because dead babies don't take your last name.

Thomas Jefferson had sex with a dead baby of a slave, only once.

I think he even realized how wrong that was.

John Hancock attempted to have sex with a dead baby in the town square in Boston.

It didn't go over so well, hence the saying: John Hancock should be known as John limpcock.

K-Mart used to sell dead babies during their blue light special.

It was one of those great things from the 80's you always remember.

The smell of dead babies smells like shit, rotten meat and talcum powder.

I wish they would make a scented candle like that.

How can you tell if your neighbor has a couple of extra dead babies in their house?

Because I'm usually there.

If you're having sex with a dead baby and a mountain lion attacks, what do you do?

Run and hold onto your dead baby by the neck. The neck of a baby is the best grip you can have.

When searching for live babies to kidnap, kill, have sex with and eat, what is the best strategy?

Use a Vietnam dead baby mail order catalog. It's a lot easier then crawling into your neighbor's window.

When stuffing a dead baby with whole cranberries, how many will fit in its ass?

Thirty Two.

The earliest game of baseball had dead babies used as the bases.

I guess that's why it used to be America's favorite past time.

When having a threesome with two dead babies, what's the rule.

Always share the same amount of time with both of them because you don't want to make either one jealous.

How much anal lube should you use when having sex with a dead baby?

A lot, you don't want to rip its asshole off.

How do you keep a dead babies skin from drying up?

Lots and lots of sperm.

When making a dead baby chandelier, what's the number one rule you should always remember?

Never forget to ground it.

How many dead baby brains does it take to fill a hippopotamus?

I couldn't tell you. I wouldn't waste that many dead baby brains on a hippo.

How much dead baby blood does it take to make a lava lamp?

Six ounces. Just don't forget to add oil, otherwise it's just a warm beverage.

How many cans of Coke can you stick in a dead babies ass?

I don't know, I couldn't even get one to fit.

When ordering a Russian mail order bride, always make sure she brings her dead babies with her.

Because everyone knows Russian men only have sex with them but never eat them and everyone knows it's not good to waste food.

What does a Cuban dead baby boy taste like?

Like a Cuban sandwich with a hint of hickory.

When making a Cuban sandwich out of dead baby meat, what should you always remember?

Don't forget the pickles.

Why do dead baby boys taste like hickory?

I think it exudes out of the marrow.

Why do dead baby girls taste like throw up?

No one knows. Scientists and chef's have puzzled over this question for centuries.

9 - DEAD BABIES, DEAD BABIES, DEAD BABIES

When dismembering dead babies, what is the number one thing to always do with the body parts?

Always separate the girls from the boys. No one wants to have a good meal ruined with the taste of throw up.

When crushing up dead baby bones to make a delicious hummus, what's the rule?

The finer the powder, the sweeter the taste.

How many dead baby carcasses would it take to make electricity for a town of three thousand people?

Way too many to waste, I suggest solar power myself.

What do you do with the left over fingers of a dead baby after carving it up for Thanksgiving?

Keep them, I'm sure you've heard of finger foods.

Dead babies are a lot easier to keep then dead prostitutes.

This isn't a joke, just stating a fact.

What's the difference between eating a dead baby and eating a dead prostitute?

You can eat a dead baby at one sitting, a dead prostitute takes a month.

What's it like, when you kill a prostitute and gut her, only to find a dead baby inside?

Like finding the toy surprise at the bottom of a box of Cracker Jack's!

How many prostitutes do you have to kill, trying to find a dead baby inside one of them?

About three, it's more like a shell game then anything else.

If TV game shows gave away dead babies as well as money, what would the contestant pick?

Depends on the money, dead babies only cost two grand each.

If an interracial couple had their choice of eating a dead white baby or a black dead baby, what would they choose?

White, because nobody really likes dark meat.

If an interracial couple wanted to have sex with a dead baby, what color would it be?

Green. Everyone knows the white couples get the fresh ones.

If a dead baby is cooked like Chinese cuisine, and another is cooked like Italian, which cuisine would leave the customer more hungry?

Neither, everyone knows if you eat a dead baby, you want more in thirty minutes.

If Spencer Pratt, Heidi Montag's husband stuck a dead baby in his ass for media attention, what would happen?

Not much, Spencer already has enough shit in his ass.

Now if Heidi Montag stuck a dead baby in her ass, what would happen?

Cover of People, Us and Variety and Spencer Pratt would try to take credit for it.

How many dead babies did Heidi Montag dissolve, dismember and use to make her self prettier?

With that much exposure, you're allowed ten dead baby bodies and one manatee.

If Spencer Pratt fucked and ate a dead baby on the steps of Congress while burning the American flag while singing the Russian anthem, what would happen?

Nothing would happen unless Heidi Montag was blowing a donkey in the background.

How many dead babies does it take to filibuster a law in Congress?

Dead babies can't filibuster a law but the Republicans can, who fuck them.

Don't eat the Olive Garden's Dead Baby surprise, even if they're advertising it.

The surprise is, there's not much dead baby and it's flashed frozen before it gets to you.

Applebee's has a special where you get one dead baby appetizer, two dead baby entrée's and a dessert made with dead baby innards for twenty dollars.

No matter how hard they try, it still tastes like crap.

Harley Davidson used to make their leather seats out of dead babies in the 60's.

Those were the fucking days.

Honda tried to make their motorcycle seats out of dead babies in the eighties.

Can't blame them, they were the cushiest seats you ever placed your genitals on.

David Hasslehoff ate a dead baby burger when he was shit faced drunk and his daughter video taped it and stuck it on you tube.

I've never seen a tastier burger before in my life.

Busch Gardens has a new ride called Dead Baby Rollercoaster. Have you ridden it yet?

It's not really worth the line, you don't get to eat it or fuck it but the picture at the end is pretty cool.

Hooter's actually made and produced a dead baby comic co-starring a hooter's waitress. So what was the problem?

She never fucked or ate the dead baby and it was more of a sidekick.

If an Islamic terrorist used dead babies as explosives, what would happen?

A lot more fucking buildings would blow up and nobody would care.

They Fonz stuck his thumb up, more dead baby asses then you can ever think of, what is the result?

AAAaaaaaaa!

Ritchie Cunningham never fucked a dead baby on the set of Happy Days. Want to know why?

Henry Winkler wouldn't share.

Jim Belushi overdosed on dead baby powdered bone fragments during the high of his career. Why?

No one told him to make it baby powder fine.

Mik Jagger and Keith Richards used to shoot up dead baby blood before every concert. Do you know why?

I don't know but their still alive today.

The sixty's was about free love and experimentation, so what went wrong?

Not enough dead babies since everyone went on the pill.

If you shoot dead baby marrow into your eye to get off, how hard are you going to get off?

Really fucking hard! A little or a lot, it's all the same.

I freebased my 1st dead baby eyeball last week and I'm still feeling it.

This isn't a joke; I just needed to tell you.

If you trade two grams of dehydrated dead baby eyeballs for coke, how much coke do you get?

I don't know, my coke dealer just had to run to the pawnshop.

I tried to buy some powdered dead baby eyeballs from my Columbian drug dealer and he was disgusted by the fact.

The fact was, he shot it all himself and didn't have any to sell.

How high would you get from snorting a dead prostitute's eyeballs?

No where near as a dead baby eyeballs.

Gatorade is a corporate shill that sells shit they make NFL teams drink and splash on coaches and teams because they get paid to do it.

Imagine if they used dead baby blood. Every game would be like the Superbowl and the players would actually drink it and like it.

Wendy's tried to make a dead baby sandwich but it failed so they took it off the menu.

Wendy's has never been known to make anything taste good.

Burger King is the only company that made a decent dead baby burger.

It's not because it was flame broiled and not because they claimed it was an angus dead baby, but because they used mayonnaise.

Checkers tried to sell us dead baby wings. They used dead baby arms and coated them with sauce and fried them in oil and even dismembered the arms into sections. Why doesn't it sell better then it should?

Because it was fried in the same oil as their potatoes and who wants their dead baby wings to taste like potatoes.

Golden Coral started to add dead baby parts to its buffet.

I always liked Golden Coral.

JC Penny began selling double stitched dead baby skin for all of their clothes. I never bought any. Why?

I don't care how fat the dead baby is, I could never fit in their jeans.

If you take a dead baby and skin it and make yourselves a pair of gloves, what can you say about it?

It's as luxurious as a Lexus and as stylish as a Gucci bag.

Luxury is saying, yes, this is American made dead baby and...

No animals were harmed.

PETA loves dead babies.

I only know this because they order from me twice a week.

Pamela Anderson eats and has sex with dead babies, twice a week.

PETA is cool with it because they don't have fur.

PETA loves dead, really dead babies. Why?

Because no matter how hard you club a dead baby, they can never look as cute as your clubbing a seal.

The only difference between clubbing a dead baby seal and a dead baby is...

You feel bad for the baby seal.

If you had a chance to kill, eat and fuck a dead baby and another chance to kill, eat and fuck a dead baby polar bear, what would you choose?

The dead baby polar bear. Only because we have all killed, fucked and ate a dead baby.

I put a dead baby on lay a way at K-mart for Christmas because it was on sale.

I waited too long and it was totally green when I finally got it but the positive point was... I didn't have to use lubrication.

If you roll a dead baby around in flour, what are you looking for?

The wet spots.

If you were to make dead baby sandwiches and have three people to eat two of the sandwiches... what happens?

One goes hungry.

Playstation 3 wanted to make an action adventure game using dead babies.

They didn't release it because no one really wants to play a game that is too close to reality.

10 - DEAD BABY AL LA CARTE

The new Rock Band video game has dead babies performing instead of make-pretend rock stars.

Rock Band rocks!

If you were to stuff half a dead baby into your jockstrap before playing a high school football game, what would happen?

You'd get a scholarship, Fuck several of the cheerleaders at the same time and win the game for your high school.

I found a dead baby in a parking lot once.

You can easily say it was my lucky day.

I found a dead baby floating in a pool once but a woman said it was hers so I let her keep it.

I could tell it was hers by the way she was French kissing it.

Dr. Joyce Meyers is a minister to a highly respected ministry.

She's made so much money even the devil can't keep up with the dead babies she eats.

Satan made a deal with Joyce Meyers so she can make millions in the name of God while pretending she's holier then thou.

Its worked so far. She can eat as many dead babies as she wants and not gain a pound.

Creflow Dollar has been working with the Lord of Darkness for years now.

Even the Government wants his IRS portfolio on dead babies to wine exemptions.

Creflow Dollar has been trying to have sex with dead rotten babies for years.

When the Lord strikes your cock impotent, he really does a number on you.

Creflow Dollar has been begging his church to give him more money to buy dead Vietnamese babies so he can fuck them in the ass.

It's because everyone knows a Vietnamese dead baby costs almost double as an American dead baby.

Joyce Meyer tried having sex with a dead baby once. It didn't work out.

Because the stupid bitch couldn't figure out how to strap on a strap on.

I had a picket line outside my house for over three months now but I just got them to leave.

Sometimes I forget to send my member's coupons for buy one dead baby and get the second one half off.

I found a dead baby under my bed last week.

I guess my wife left it there to surprise me for my birthday.

How many dead babies does it take to make a good Irish stew?

None, everyone knows the Irish bake their dead babies; because a stew would be a waste.

The rarest dead baby on the planet is an Eskimo dead baby? What to know why?

Who wants to eat or fuck something that's frozen.

The Australians like to marinate their dead babies in the pouch of a Kangaroo.

I don't know what they call it but I know it's going to taste good.

The Japanese marinate their dead babies in sake for 6 months before they sell the sake to rich businessmen. Do you want to know what it tastes like?

I don't know, I could never spend that much money on the nectar of the gods.

Marvel Comics tried to release a comic book series about the adventures of a dead baby. It sold out for the 1st issue and then slowly dropped off till no one bought it anymore.

Every issue just had the baby rotting and even though it sounds exciting, it isn't.

DC Comics had an issue where Superman married a dead baby. He divorced it a couple of issues later. Then Superman married Lois Lane but was divorced six issued after.

Batman knew it wouldn't last because who can compete against an ex who could do everything.

Robin always hated Batman for not sharing his dead baby stash with him in the Batcave.

I mean who can blame him? I'd be pissed too.

Aquaman never had the chance to fuck a dead baby.

I mean really? Who's going to throw precious cargo into the sea?

Dead babies can bring a smile to your lips and an erection in your pants.

It's more of a reality then just wishful thinking.

NASA wanted to shoot dead babies into space but PETA was against it.

NASA sent chimpanzees instead.

Chimpanzees eat their dead babies; they don't fuck them.

I guess we really have evolved.

Darwin tried not to eat a dead baby because he believed in evolution and he knew chimps ate their young.

He realized when he was fucking one, that if he ate it, he evolved.

What do you do if you see an octopus eating a dead baby at Sea World?

Take a lot of pictures! Video if you have it!

Have you tried the new caramel covered dead baby on a stick?

No? You should, they're only around on Halloween.

Did you hear about the woman who kept a dead baby in her uterus for over 40 years?

Safer then a bank and close to her heart!

So, this woman had a dead baby inside her uterus for over 40 years; had a simple surgical procedure to remove it. What was the first thing they did when they removed it?

The Head Surgeon put it on the operating table next to her and began fucking the Hell out of it.

No one wants to hear about a 40-year-old virgin except in a movie.

Did you ever see a horror comedy movie called Frankenhooker?

Me neither, it didn't have any dead baby sex in it.

Have you heard of that awesome horror dvd company called Unearthed Films?

I knew you did, their the 1st company to make a movie with dead baby fucking in it.

The movie Slow Torture Puke Chamber from Unearthed Films has a man fucking a dead baby. What is the highlight of the film?

After fucking it, he throws up on it and fucks it some more. Why can't Steven Speilberg and George Lucas give the people what they want?

Dead baby fucking was opted out of the summer Olympics why?

They didn't want it to outshine the gymnastics competition.

The last winter Olympics was great because they tried to set a dead baby on fire and tried to carry it to set the ceremonial fire at the opening of it. Why didn't it work?

Dead babies don't have enough hair to run a block, much less half way across the world.

The police found a stash of a hundred babies, set up in variations of the Karma Sutra in a man's basement. What does that mean?

He was working on the coolest picture book of sexual positions the world has ever seen.

UPS has a strict rule for shipping rotten dead babies round the world. Know what it is?

Always use a trash bag and plenty of Styrofoam peanuts.

The United States Postal Service refuses to ship dead babies internationally. What should you do?

You did just read the instructions above...
always ship UPS.

Fed Ex is trying to keep up with UPS and they
have relaxed their rules on shipping dead babies.
Fed Ex doesn't make you use a trash bag to ship
them.

I'll never use Fed Ex, part of the fun is stuffing
them into trash bags.

Adult Friend Finder doesn't have a section in
their fetishes for dead baby fucking. Want to
know why?

The people running it are Jehovah's Witnesses.

I had a Jehovah's Witness knock on my door
while I was fucking two dead babies while
talking dirty to another on my recliner. Why
didn't I answer the door?

I didn't want to ruin my mojo.

The Jehovah's Witness kept banging on my door
and I just kept banging on my dead kids. Why

did I not answer the door, even after ten minutes of knocking?

I only had so much lube.

11 - DEAD BABIES IN GOVERNMENT

Michael Vick got a call from President Obama, what did they talk about?

Michael Vick's failed dead baby fighting ring and Obama's new robot dead baby fighting competition made by the Defense Department with cybernetic robots and dead baby flesh. Talk about wanting to be a fly on the wall.

So, President Obama is using the Defense Dept. to make a cybernetic dead baby-fighting competition using taxpayers dollars.

Best use of Government money yet!

So, the Government's, cybernetic dead baby fighting competition is going to happen in twelve months and if not, it will be carried onto the next President if he doesn't finish it in time. My question is? Who is going to fuck all of those cybernetic dead babies after they loose?

Some lucky individual, that's who!

Obama has talked about getting America out of the recession.

This cybernetic dead baby fighting competition is definitely in the right direction.

So I went to a support group due to my addiction of fucking and eating dead babies. I left feeling worse.

Not only did they not have any dead babies to fuck, they tried to serve me coffee cake!

Macy's tried to have a dead baby Thanksgiving Day Parade but it didn't work out.

Macy's just didn't understand that Helium escapes out of a dead babies ass when you try fill them up and corks really don't work.

My friend Rhett Rushing found a dead baby on the side of the road. He called me first to find out what to do, so I told him.

Run to the nearest sex shop to buy lingerie and lube, then to Radio Shack for batteries for his camera and how to set up a webcam. Then I told him to go to Publix for a bunch of bananas. Why the bananas? After that much fucking, he's going to need as much potassium as he can get, to get his energy back up.

What do you call a dead baby covered in slime and filth, rotting in a corner?

Your awesome blind date.

What do you call a bloody dead baby stuck on a pole?

A birdfeeder.

What do you call a dead baby sitting on your front doorway?

A blessing.

What do you call a dead baby that has been decapitated and dismembered and hidden around your yard?

An Easter egg hunt.

What do you call a dead baby without any eyes?

Blind.

What do you call a dead baby stuffed in your mailbox?

A special delivery.

What do you call a dead baby that doesn't have any legs?

Half an entrée.

What do you call a naked dead baby laying on a polar bear rug?

A photoshoot.

What do you call a dead baby with hypodermic needles stuck in every inch of its body?

A porcupine.

What do you call a dead baby tied to your car by a piece of rope?

The start of a wonderful marriage.

What do you call, finding a dead baby at the beach?

Lucky.

What do you do when you find a dead baby at a club?

Give it a roofie and quickly call a cab.

What do you call a dead baby being thrown off the Empire State Building?

A waste of good food.

What do you call a dead baby when its cheeks have been ripped apart to the back of the jaw.

A sex worker.

What can you do with a dead baby in the back seat of your car?

Anything you want. The possibilities are endless.

What do you call a rotten dead baby that is being picked apart by buzzards?

A rotten shame.

When you dehydrate a dead baby with a dehydrator. What do you call it?

Beef jerky.

What do you call a dead baby dressed up in a suit and tie?

Sexy and available.

How many dead babies does it take to please a man?

One, unless he can talk it into a threesome.

What do you call a dead baby floating in space?

A sexy, edible satellite.

How many dead babies did Jack the Ripper have?

None, that's why he had to kill prostitutes.

What do you call making whiskey out of dead baby blood?

A great invention.

How many dead babies does it take to keep a two hundred and fifty pound man afloat in a pool?

Five, one for each arm and leg and the last one he gets to fuck.

When collecting dead babies and you want to store them, how should you?

Suck the blood out of them and then encase them in carbonite.

How many dead baby slushies can you make out of five dead babies?

Enough for everyone in your family to have one.

A romance with a dead baby is like being in love for the 1st time.

You just can't wait to take its virginity.

Dead babies are good for almost everything that ails you. Do you know what it doesn't help you with?

Bunions. No matter how many times you rub you feet on them, it still doesn't do anything except give you an erection.

How many credit card miles do you need to exchange for a dead baby?

I don't know, I don't use my credit card that much.

Have you ever been to a dead baby-dating site?

You should, all you need for pictures is candy.

Have you seen the new porno called Dead Baby Ass Fuckers #12?

You should; it's a masterpiece.

How many dead babies can you safely cook in your oven?

Two… just two.

When cooking a dead baby, where should you stick the meat thermometer?

Wherever you want… use your imagination.

How many dead babies can you legally bring across the border from Mexico?

Up to four and a half without a prescription.

How many dead babies can you bring on a plane if you're traveling internationally?

As many as you can stuff in your carry on luggage.

How many dead babies can you have sex with without feeling guilty?

I don't know, I never feel guilty about that.

How many teeth can you pull out of a dead babies mouth?

Well, if you can pull a tooth out, it's not a dead baby. It's a dead child so you're sicker then I thought.

How come you can never find a dead baby on the side of the road anymore?

They're are too many truckers that know what they're looking for nowadays.

How many ounces of dead baby brains does it take to fill a quart?

Four of they're are fresh, six if they're rotten.

How many dead babies does it take to ruin a party?

None. Everyone knows a dead baby makes the party.

Have you ever made a pair of underwear using dead baby skin?

You should, it's like having a party in your pants.

How many dead babies does it take to fill a wheelbarrow?

I don't know, I can't stop eating them before I fill it up.

What's the difference between a polar bear and a dead baby?

Polar bears are close to extinction.

What do you do if you run out of dead baby meat while serving a party of four?

Serve dead puppy and hope no ones taste buds are that refined.

Shakespeare wrote Othello after having sex with a dead baby.

Talk about inspiration!

When bleeding a dead baby to make beef jerky, what should you always do?

Hang it upside down and squeeze it from the feet towards the throat. It's not really a joke but more of a fact.

If you stick a baby in a blender, what should you never forget?

Put on the lid. You don't want to spend hours cleaning up your kitchen.

When serving dead baby to guests during New Years Eve, what should you never forget?

To put the TV on and watch the ball drop.

12 - MORE FAMOUS PEOPLE WITH DEAD BABIES

Rock Hudson used to make love to dead babies every day of his natural life.

I don't know how he caught AID's from one so use protection from now on.

Kirk Douglas once ate seven dead babies a day to prepare for the movie Spartacus.

Now that's preparing for a roll.

Robert DeNiro stuffed a dead baby up his ass every day to prepare for his roll in Raging Bull.

The eighties was a weird time to prepare for a roll in a movie.

Brett Michaels uses dead baby hair to cover his bald spot with a bandana holding it into place.

I never liked Poison or Brett Michaels but at least I respect him now.

I just found out that Poison's song, Talk Dirty To Me, Brett Michaels was actually singing about a dead baby when he wrote that song.

I always hated that song but now I think it's a nice little ditty.

KISS's song Lick It Up, was actually about licking up the excrement that leaked out of a dead babies ass as it rotted in a corner.

For some odd reason, I still hate that song.

Bruce Jenner, the Olympic gold medal winner had plastic surgery and had his face replaced with dead baby skin.

Even though he's freakish looking now, he has an allure he didn't have before.

Albert Einstein was one of the greatest minds of the nineteenth century. That is, until we found out he fucked and ate dead babies.

Now he's the greatest mind of all time.

Jeffrey Dahmer was a sick and twisted individual who had gay sex with male corpses and when he was busted, he got life in prison.

He should have stuck with dead babies. I hear you get a medal when arrested.

Did you hear about the Buddhist Temple where they found over one thousand dead babies?

That must have been one Hell of a Chinese Buffet!

What happens when you lick a dead baby, besides the erection you get?

Your mouth drools and you turn on the oven.

How many men want to have sex with dead babies?

All of them, they just won't ever tell you.

How many women want to have sex with a dead baby?

Not many, it's hard to strap on a dildo to something so slippery and small.

If the Government made dead babies the prime food source of America, it would save the economy, why?

It's renewable, delicious and fun for everyone.

If you were to use a dead baby as a yard dart target, what would happen?

Your neighbors would never leave and the damn grandkids would want to come over all the time.

If you were to use a dead baby as a dartboard, what would happen?

Best dang game of darts you will ever play in your life.

If you fill up a dead babies ass with water, what is it called?

A super soaker.

If you fill up a dead babies ass with water a second time, what can you call it?

A canteen.

How many dead babies does Hillary Rodham Clinton eat for breakfast?

Not enough, she's still an uptight bitch.

Carrot Top has been eating and having sex with dead babies for years now. Funny thing is...

It's only with girl babies. I guess he likes the taste of throw up.

When cooking a dead baby girl to consume, how do you disguise the taste of throw up?

You can't. Believe me, I tried everything.

If your neighbor has a dead baby and your grandmother has a dead baby and one of them is using it for sex and the other for a nice dinner, which one is it?

It's a trick question because it depends on who has the girl.

If dead baby boys are mostly sold for eating and girl dead babies are mostly sold for sex, which one is better?

The dead baby boys. Because you can fuck them and eat them. Girl dead babies taste like throw up and always leave an aftertaste in your mouth for a week.

Why are dead baby boys so delicious?

I don't know either... they just are.

How many dead babies can you fit into a Volkswagen Bug?

Seventy-three if you include the dismembered ones in the glove compartment.

North Korea has a law where you can't eat or have sex with any dead babies, no matter what gender they are.

Who would have guessed the North Koreans actually uphold equal rights laws.

So, have you heard that you can't eat or have sex with any dead babies in North Korea at all.

Worst vacation spot ever!

If Jimmy Carter ate and then had sex with a dead baby during his presidency, what would have happened?

He would have been liked just a little bit more.

If you stick you dick in a dead babies nose, what would you call it?

A very, very tight fit.

If your neighbors are making too much noise, what should you do?

Cut your dead babies big toes off and stick them in your ears. It works for me.

If you find a mountain lion eating a dead baby, what should you do?

Throw rocks at it. It's not a bear and dead babies are worth a two thousand bucks each!

If you take a baby into out of space and stick it into the escape hatch and eject it, what do you get?

A burst of baby guts and an erection.

Astronauts train for years so they can bring a dead baby into space just to fuck and not to eat.

Talk about fucking willpower.

Michael Jackson had a treasure trove of dead babies. Why did he have to molest a couple of live boys now and then?

Because every now and then, he would get a hankering for something older.

Michael Jackson would fill up his merry go round by duct-taping dead babies to the horses. What was the problem?

Vultures. If it wasn't for the vultures, it would be better then Disney land.

Did you know Michael Jackson's glove wasn't covered in sparkles, it was dead baby irises.

Yeah, I didn't know they glowed that bright either.

Michael Jackson's song Beat It was about beating dead babies. Did you know that?

Me neither but I just saw the newest remake of his video after he died and I do have to say... best video ever!

Do you think Michael Jackson ever let his pet chimpanzee molest the dead babies he kept in his basement?

Hell no! Who wants monkey cum all over their food!

Michael Jackson practiced the Moonwalk over a layer of dead babies for the Grammy's.

It must have been the coolest practice ever.

Michael Jackson used a couple of dead babies for his skin whitening procedures. What did the Doctor say to him?

"You're a lucky son of a bitch."

Did you know that a major component of spray tan is blended African baby skin?

They don't use the insides because the tan doesn't go that deep.

13 - DISGUSTING DEAD BABIES

What are more fun then a barrel of monkeys?

A barrel of K-Y filled, with dead babies in lingerie.

What's more fun then a barrel of K-Y filled with dead babies in lingerie?

Nothing.

What did the miner say when a plane blew up and mutilated dead babies poured from the sky all over Kentucky?

"Boys, there's gold in them there hills!"

How many dead babies does it take to calm down a riot in a prison?

None, everyone knows hetero faggots don't fuck dead babies.

If you stroke your wife with a dead baby, what is it called?

Foreplay.

If your wife strokes you with a dead baby, what is it called?

Sex.

How many teeth can you pull out of a dead baby's mouth?

None, they haven't grown them yet.

How hard do you have to kick a dead baby to get it into your neighbor's back yard.

Pretty hard.

How many dead Cuban babies does it take to make a foot long Cuban sandwich?

Only one.

How hard is it to run from the cops while carrying three dead babies?

I don't know so lets hope we never have to find out.

Busch Gardens has a new ride where you straddle a dead baby and it spins you around for a couple of minutes.

I know, weirdest way to get an erection ever.

Dead baby strip bars are pretty lame because they can't dance.

But the lap dances are the best because they can't slap your hands away.

Skydiving with a dead baby strapped to your pack is an easy way to commit suicide.

But running with a dead baby strapped to your crotch is an easy way to achieve orgasm.

Lady Gaga wore an outfit of dead babies to the Grammy Awards. What did people notice the most?

Her shoes.

Janet Jackson wore the same outfit of dead babies to the MTV Awards. What did everyone say after?

That she's a racist since the dead babies were white.

If dead baby boys taste like hickory and dead baby girls taste like throw up, what do black dead baby boys and black dead baby girls taste like?

Black dead baby boys tastes like hickory with a hint of brown sugar and black dead baby girls taste like throw up with a hint of shit.

If boys taste better then girls and black babies boys have a hint of brown sugar, what does that mean for every other race of dead babies?

I don't know either but it's going to be fun finding out.

If you're in the middle of a swingers party and someone breaks out a dead baby, what's going to happen?

Somebody's wife is going to really get jealous.

What's going to hurt less, your wife or husband leaving you for a dead baby or being left for the opposite sex?

The dead baby, because at least you know you didn't turn them gay.

If Mr. Rogers was having sex with a dead baby in imagination land and you sat there, wanting to have sex with a dead baby while he did it, what would happen?

He would turn to you and say, "You know, I think everybody longs to be loved, and longs to know that he or she is lovable. And, consequently, the greatest thing that we can do is to help somebody know that they're loved and capable of loving."

Then he would proceed to fuck a dead baby in front of you.

People refuse to admit the fun you can have with a dead baby that loves sex.

It's only because everyone thinks they just want to be eaten.

Dead babies come and go and leave us with a taste in our mouth.

It's a taste we all hanker for and a desire we all want to plunge into.

Space is called the final frontier…

Until you stick your dick into something dead and young.

Elephants have been taught to fuck dead baby Indian kids in the ass in front of crowds of people.

Damn, I wish I had a season ticket.

Using dead babies for chum to fish for sharks is not the best way to do it.

You can catch everything else with bull balls but you only catch third grade teachers with dead babies.

Vultures only eat dead babies when they can find them. Why?

It's because the third grade teachers don't drag them behind their cars anymore.

If you use four dead babies to get you off and then use three dead babies to make you feel good about yourself. How many dead babies do you need to make you feel positive about yourself?

Only one… One dead baby makes you realize the world is how it should be.

If you found a dead baby in the middle of the road, what would you think?

That your world is becoming better!

If you drink soup, out of a hollowed baby skull, what's the problem?

Nothing, if it's really good soup!

If you hollow out a dead babies body, to drink from like a canteen and you find yourself in the desert, thirsty. What do you do?

Drink from its toes. Everyone knows, they brain soaks up the liquid.

If... Atari Space Invaders used dead babies instead of space invaders.

We would still be playing it.

If Michael Crichton wrote about dead babies instead dinosaurs...

Jurassic Park would have been totally awesome!

If Shakespeare wrote the Murders In The Rue Morgue, about dead babies instead of a gorilla killing people…

It would still be in the New York Times Best Sellers list.

Some people have never eaten or fucked a dead baby and refuse to even admit they would, much less enjoy it.

Most people just enjoy eating and fucking dead puppies. I don't know why… probably because they have fur, taste like cinnamon and are adorable.

Why would someone want to fuck a dead puppy and then eat them?

I guess racism comes in all shapes and sizes!

Not many people want to fuck and eat a dead kittens instead of a dead baby.

It's not only their bones, but their hair gets everywhere.

What's easier, to stuff… a dead baby up your ass or a dead kitten?

Dead babies all the way. Dead kittens have claws!

If Richard Gere stuffed a dead baby up his ass, shit it out and then stuffed a dead gerbil up his ass. What is the sexiest thing up his ass?

The dead baby! Gerbil hair catches the shit in your colon as it comes out.

How much shit does a dead baby cover itself as it leaves your asshole if you stuck it in there, in the 1st place?

None, the natural lubricant works for everyone.

If the Pep Boys shoved dead babies into your engine to make it run better, what would happen?

Everyone would win the Daytona 500.

If a crossing guard used a dead baby as their flag and they waved it around to make people go slower so kids can cross the road… What would happen?

The kids would go slower and the people in the cars would jerk off.

If Osama Bin Laden had sex with three dead baby camels and then ate them in front of a bunch of terrorists, what would happen?

There would be peace in the Middle East.

How many dead babies can Osama Bin Laden stuff into his turban?

Only two but they slowly leak onto his forehead, which is like air conditioning.

ABOUT THE COMPANY

UNEARTHED BOOKS

Unearthed Books is the off shoot of the horror DVD label, Unearthed Films. Normally releasing cutting edge horror, cult and gore films is now stepping into the book publishing arena. Their next book Hellucination is the true story of Stephen Biro. It can be called a memoir but it is unlike anything that has been written before.

It chronicles his childhood when he lost his faith with haunting clarity. It then moves into the drug induced fervor of his life trying to find God using LSD and Nitrous Oxide. Before he could find God, he found the Devil instead. Hallucinations began to blend into the real world as people became possessed around him. Friends and acquaintances came out of the word work, explaining to him their angels, antichrists and even god himself. That's when the Satan went full force at him and took him into the nether realms of insanity, trying to confuse and manipulate him into pure blasphemy.

That's when the Lord showed up. Showing him, who he truly is. Then sending him down into Hell to see what awaited him there. A truly harrowing experience not be taken lightly.

It's the next book From Unearthed Books. Stay Tuned

40666731R00083